STARS OF SPORTS

ALEX MORGAN

SOCCER CHAMPION

■■▌by Shane Frederick

CAPSTONE PRESS

Stars of Sports is published by Capstone Press, an imprint of Capstone.
1710 Roe Crest Drive, North Mankato, Minnesota 56003
www.capstonepub.com

Library of Congress Cataloging-in-Publication Data
Names: Chandler, Matt, author.
Title: Alex Morgan : soccer champion / Matt Chandler.
Description: North Mankato : Capstone Press, 2020. | Series: Stars of
    sports | Includes bibliographical references and index. | Audience: Ages
    8-11 | Audience: Grades 4-6 | Summary: "Alex Morgan first joined a
    soccer team when she was 14 years old, quickly impressing her peers and
    coaches with her skills. From there, she grew to become a world-class
    soccer player, reaching incredible heights including a FIFA Women's
    World Cup championship and an Olympic gold medal. Learn about Alex's
    rise in soccer in this electric biography in the Stars of Sports
    series"-- Provided by publisher.
Identifiers: LCCN 2019039814 (print) | LCCN 2019039815 (ebook) | ISBN
    9781543591682 (hardcover) | ISBN 9781543591835 (pdf)
Subjects: LCSH: Morgan, Alex (Alexandra Patricia), 1989---Juvenile
    literature. | Women soccer players--United States--Biography--Juvenile
    literature.
Classification: LCC GV942.7.M673 C43 2020 (print) | LCC GV942.7.M673
    (ebook) | DDC 796.334092 [B]--dc23
LC record available at https://lccn.loc.gov/2019039814
LC ebook record available at https://lccn.loc.gov/2019039815

Editorial Credits
Editor: Hank Musolf; Designer: Ashlee Suker; Media Researcher: Eric Gohl;
Production Specialist: Laura Manthe

Image Credits
Getty Images: Collegiate Images, 11, 13, Stringer/Jesse Grant, 27; Newscom: Cal
Sport Media/Alan Schwartz, 15, Cal Sport Media/Simon Bellis, 5, El Mercurio
de Chile/Rolando Oyarzun, 7, Icon SMI/Scott Bales, 9, Icon SMI/YCJ/Andy
Mead, 14, Icon Sportswire/Andrew Dieb, 19, Icon Sportswire/Joe Petro, 17, Icon
Sportswire/Marc Piscotty, 21, Icon Sportswire/Robin Alam, cover, 20, ZUMA Press/
Andrew Chin, 28, ZUMA Press/Ken Hawkins, 16, ZUMA Press/Mark Smith, 23;
Shutterstock: EFKS, 1, Lev Radin, 24

All internet sites appearing in back matter were available and accurate when this
book was sent to press.

Direct Quotations
Pages 25, from June 12, 2019, ESPN article "USWNT's Alex Morgan taking on
leading role she was born to play", https://www.espn.com
Page 27, from June 13, 2018. USA Today article "Alex Morgan gives acting a go,
readies for qualifying", https://www.usatoday.com

Printed in the United States of America.
PA99

TABLE OF CONTENTS

AN OLYMPIC HERO 4

CHAPTER ONE
FUTURE SOCCER STAR 6

CHAPTER TWO
COLLEGE STAR 10

CHAPTER THREE
GOING PRO 14

CHAPTER FOUR
WOMEN'S NATIONAL TEAM 20

CHAPTER FIVE
BRIGHT FUTURE 26

TIMELINE 29
GLOSSARY 30
READ MORE 31
INTERNET SITES 31
INDEX 32

Glossary terms are **BOLD** on first use.

AN OLYMPIC HERO

The United States women's soccer team was tied with Canada. It was the 2012 Summer Olympics. The score was 3-3. The winner would advance to the gold-medal match. Time was running out. With one last chance to score, the Americans closed in.

American Abby Wambach sent a long pass out. It went to the corner to teammate Heather O'Reilly. Alex Morgan slid in to the front of the goal. She was in perfect position. O'Reilly sent a high kick toward Morgan. The 23-year-old forward leaped in the air. She delivered a perfect **header.** The ball shot just past the arms of the goalkeeper. It went into the net. The Americans won, and Morgan was an Olympic hero!

Morgan defends the ball in the 2012 Olympic Games. 〉〉〉

CHAPTER ONE

FUTURE SOCCER STAR

Alex Morgan was born in San Dimas, California, on July 2, 1989. She has two older sisters. She was raised in Diamond Bar, California.

Today Morgan is considered a great soccer player. But growing up, soccer was just one sport she played. She also played softball, basketball, and volleyball. Playing sports helped her build confidence. They also helped her make friends. Morgan said she never imagined playing soccer professionally when she began playing. She also didn't imagine winning a gold medal.

FACT

When she was a child growing up in California, Morgan had a pet rat.

>>> Morgan (right) charges during the 2008 Women's World Cup.

"On the field, I was able to hang out with kids my age, kick the ball around and just have a good time," she wrote in 2013.

Morgan didn't become really focused on soccer until she was 14 years old. She played for her high school. She also played for a club team called Cypress Elite.

TEEN SENSATION

It takes **stamina** to play soccer. Morgan ran track in high school. She earned a Varsity letter on her track team. Running helped her build stamina for soccer. She was also on her school's volleyball team.

Morgan missed her senior season. She suffered a torn **ACL**, a ligament in the knee. She was already seen as an **elite** soccer player. She earned a **scholarship** to play soccer. She would play at the University of California at Berkeley.

Morgan worked hard to recover from her injury. She was out for five months. She had to wear a brace on her injured knee. Morgan's injury didn't bother the coaches. When she recovered fully, the 17-year-old Morgan got great news. The coaches selected her to join the under-20 Women's National Team!

FACT

Morgan was cut from the first club team she tried out for when she was 13.

>>> Morgan plays for the U.S. under-17 Women's National Team.

CHAPTER TWO

COLLEGE STAR

Morgan suffered a sprained ankle that delayed the start of her college career. She still wore a knee brace from her injury. Once she recovered, she was finally ready to play. She made moving from high school to college look easy.

Morgan played for the Golden Bears in the 2007 season. She earned her first start in the sixth game of the season. The game was scoreless at the 53-minute mark. Morgan broke through. She collected a pass from teammate McKenna-Louise McKetty. She knocked the ball past Aztec goaltender Aubrey Southwick. The ball went into the net for the 1-0 lead!

Morgan scored eight goals and 18 points in 2007. She was the top scorer on her team. The Golden Bears earned a spot in the National Collegiate Athletic Association (NCAA) tournament.

>>> Morgan celebrates after scoring for the Golden Bears.

The first round of the tournament was against Santa Clara. Morgan delivered an **assist** in a 2-0 win. Her biggest moment came at the end of the second round. There were less than two minutes remaining. The Golden Bears trailed Stanford 1-0. Their season was on the line. Morgan came through. She delivered a header past Stanford goalkeeper Erica Holland. She tied the game and forced overtime!

TOP SCORER

Morgan continued to improve in college. She led team scores for the next three seasons. Morgan's best year in college was her junior year. She put up 36 points on 14 goals and eight assists.

Morgan was ready to break those numbers in her senior year. But she was called up to the national women's team. She couldn't play in as many college games. Still, she delivered 14 goals in just 12 games. Once again, her team returned to the NCAA tournament. Morgan's team had earned a playoff spot each year she played. Her team was eliminated in her final college game. They lost to Duke 2-1 in the first round. It was time for Morgan's next challenge.

>>> Morgan's last season playing for the Golden Bears was in 2010.

CHAPTER THREE

GOING PRO

It was January 2011. The Western New York Flash made Morgan the first player chosen in the **draft**. The Flash is a team in the United Women's Soccer league. Morgan didn't walk to a podium. She didn't hug her family and friends. She didn't even know she had been drafted. Alex Morgan was 30,000 feet (9,144 meters) in the air. She was on a plane headed to China. The women's national team was going to play there.

>>> Morgan (back row, second from right) poses with her Flash teammates.

<<< Morgan chases the ball in a 2011 game.

The **rookie** scored four goals in her first season. Her team went on to win the league championship.

The Women's Professional Soccer league suspended play before the 2012 season. In February 2012, Morgan signed a new contract. She would play with the Seattle Sounders Women. With her on the team, they had a great season. Fans filled stadiums to see Morgan and her teammates. Nine out of 10 home games that season were sold out.

BECOMING A SUPERSTAR

Today Morgan is known as a soccer superstar. Morgan has earned international fame on the women's national team. Morgan has played for four American teams. In 2013, she played for the Portland Thorns. She led the Thorns to the National Women's Soccer League Championship.

〉〉〉 Morgan controls the ball playing for the Portland Thorns.

<<< Morgan attempts a goal for the Orlando Pride in a game against the Washington Spirit.

Morgan has played in more than 100 club matches. She has scored 44 goals in club play. She has won two national championships. Since 2016, Morgan has been a forward for the Orlando Pride.

FACT

Morgan earns more than $3 million per year from **endorsement** deals with companies such as Nike, McDonald's and Coca-Cola.

GOING FOR THE GOLD

Morgan collected her first Olympic gold medal with the women's national team in 2012. Japan's team had won the World Cup in 2011. The team was defending its championship win. The U.S. team defeated Japan 2-1. The Americans may not have made it if not for Morgan. The semi-final game was against Canada. She scored a heroic goal to win 4-3. Morgan scored three goals in her first Olympic Games.

Award Winner

Morgan has earned many awards and medals during her career. She was named the Player of the Year by U.S. Soccer twice. She was a finalist for the FIFA World Player of the Year. Morgan also has earned a gold and a silver medal as a member of the Women's World Cup.

〉〉〉 Morgan scores a goal in the first minute of the Olympic qualifying game against Costa Rica in 2016.

In 2016, Morgan had another chance for a gold medal. The United States Women's team faced off against Costa Rica. The game took place on February 10, 2016. Both teams were trying to qualify for the Summer Olympics.

The game began. American Carli Lloyd headed the ball toward the goal. Morgan raced up the middle. She delivered a kick past goaltender Dinnia Diaz. Morgan set a record. It was the fastest a goal was scored in the history of the U.S. women's national team. She scored only 12 seconds into the game!

The Americans returned from the 2016 Olympics without a medal. But Morgan still earned a place in the history books.

CHAPTER FOUR

WOMEN'S NATIONAL TEAM

In April 2019, the women's national team faced Australia. The match was scoreless in the fourteenth minute. Morgan raced toward the Australian goal. There were two defenders in her path. Morgan's shot aimed right between the defenders. She delivered a hard kick and scored. The crowd went wild. Morgan had scored her 100th international goal!

〉〉〉 Morgan rushes for the ball against Australia's Gema Simon on April 12, 2019.

>>> Morgan (right) celebrates after scoring her 100th goal.

Morgan is a veteran on the women's national team. She has appeared in more than 160 international matches. She also has more than 40 assists in her career. In 2011, she was on the World Cup team. She won a silver medal with them. In 2015, Morgan scored one goal in the tournament. She helped the United States take home the World Cup.

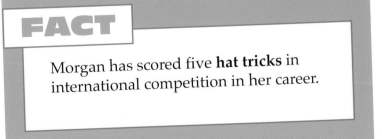

FACT

Morgan has scored five **hat tricks** in international competition in her career.

2019 WORLD CUP

Morgan saved her best performance for the next World Cup. The opening round of the 2019 World Cup was against Thailand. The United States defended its title. Morgan was unstoppable! The U.S. players set a World Cup record. They scored 13 goals in the game. Morgan tied a World Cup record with five goals.

The United States crushed Thailand 13-0. Morgan showed amazing sportsmanship. She found Thai forward Miranda Nild on the **pitch**. Nild is a fellow Berkeley graduate. She wanted to help her friend feel better after the heartbreaking loss.

Morgan and the United States team continued to impress in the World Cup. The semifinal game was against England's team. Morgan scored during the game. She was the first woman to score a goal during the World Cup on her birthday!

The United States team faced the Netherlands in the finals. The Netherlands had a defense that was prepared for Morgan. She still played well. The crowd cheered as the United States won the game 2-0. Morgan was a two-time World Cup champion!

⟩⟩⟩ Morgan celebrates with her teammates after scoring a record-tying goal during the Women's World Cup in 2019.

Off the Field

Morgan is a star on the pitch, but she has become a star off the field as well. The popularity of women's soccer has grown. So have the opportunities for its stars. Morgan is a spokesperson for some of the biggest brands in America. Morgan has written a series of children's books. She has become a **political activist**. She has also done some acting and modeling. Many soccer players retire by the time they're 35 years old. Morgan has options for her post-soccer career. Morgan is developing other opportunities for herself that has nothing to do with scoring goals.

OLYMPIC RETURN

The 2020 Summer Olympics will be held in Tokyo. It will be Morgan's third trip to the Olympic Games. The United States team has dominated the World Cup competition. Morgan and the U.S. team will be a favorite to win the gold medal.

In 2012, Morgan was one of the youngest players. This time, many of the veterans will be gone. Abby Wambach and Hope Solo are retired. Morgan will be expected to lead the team.

Morgan says she loves the pressure of competing. There is added pressure on the world stage. She remembers leaving the 2016 Olympics without a medal. "I never want to feel the way that I felt after that tournament," Morgan said. "Looking ahead [to 2020] I think we have to show our best."

CHAPTER FIVE

BRIGHT FUTURE

Morgan turned 30 years old in 2019. Fans want to know how much longer she will play. For many athletes, it depends on how healthy they are. Morgan has suffered multiple ankle injuries in her professional career. She also had the torn ACL in high school. Morgan is a top player when healthy. She has shown she can still play at a top level.

Morgan has talked a lot about how competitive she is. She also loves the game of soccer. Her fans hope these two things keep her on the pitch for a long time! In less than 10 years, Morgan has already proven to be one of the greatest soccer players in history.

Morgan (right) and actor Siena Agudong at the premiere of *Alex & Me* on May 18, 2018.

Movie Star

In 2016, Morgan took an acting role playing herself in the movie *Alex and Me*. It tells the story of a young girl inspired by the soccer star. It was released in 2018. Morgan says she took the role of actress very seriously. She hired an acting coach and worked hard to learn her new job. Morgan said she experienced many different emotions watching herself in the movie. "You're embarrassed, you're proud, you feel like you've delivered your lines well, or you've captured the emotion of a scene, or possibly not," she said.

ONE OF THE GREATS

Less than 20 women in the history of professional soccer have scored more than 100 goals in international play. Morgan is one of them. Fellow American Abby Wambach holds the record with 184 international goals. Morgan is only 30 years old, and she could play for another 10 years. Many experts believe she could retire as the all-time leading goal scorer in women's soccer.

FACT

Morgan is married to professional soccer player Servando Carrasco. The couple met when they were college students.

TIMELINE

1989 Morgan is born on July 2 in San Dimas, California.

2007 Morgan enrolls at University of California, Berkeley and joins the school soccer program.

2010 She graduates from Berkeley. The team made it to the NCAA tournament all four years she was a member.

2010 Morgan joins the Women's National Team.

2011 Morgan is drafted by the Western New York Flash to play professional soccer.

2011 Morgan is named to the FIFA Women's World Cup team. At 22, she is the youngest player on the team.

2012 Morgan wins an Olympic Gold medal as a member of the 2012 U.S. Women's Soccer team.

2012 Morgan scores her first career hat trick in a 4-0 win over Sweden at the World Cup.

2012 Morgan is named Female Athlete of the Year by U.S. Soccer.

2013 Morgan publishes her first children's book, *Saving the Team*. It becomes a *New York Times* best seller.

2015 Morgan wins first FIFA World Cup championship.

2018 Morgan stars in the movie *Alex and Me*.

2019 Morgan wins her second FIFA World Cup championship.

GLOSSARY

ASSIST (uh-SIST)—a pass that leads to a score by a teammate

DRAFT (DRAFT)—an event in which athletes are picked to join sports organizations or teams

ELITE (i-LEET)—among the best

ENDORSEMENT (in-DORS-muhnt)—the act of an athlete wearing, promoting, or using a product, often for money

HAT TRICK (HAT TRIK)—when a player scores three goals in a single game

HEADER (HED-ur)—a shot where players use their heads to hit the ball

PITCH (PITCH)—grass surface of a soccer field

POLITICAL ACTIVIST (puh-LIT-uh-kuhl AK-tuh-vist)—someone who fights for issues they believe in to encourage support or change

ROOKIE (RUK-ee)—a player who is playing his or her first year on a team

SCHOLARSHIP (SKOL-ur-ship)—money given to a student to pay for school

STAMINA (STAM-uh-nuh)—the energy and strength to keep doing something for a long time

READ MORE

Greder, Andrew. *Behind the Scenes Soccer*. Minneapolis, MN: Lerner Publications, 2019.

Pina, Andrew. *Becoming a Pro Soccer Player*. New York: Gareth Stevens, 2015.

Terrell, Brandon. *Soccer Showdown: U.S. Women's Stunning 1999 World Cup Win*. North Mankato, MN: Capstone Press, 2019.

INTERNET SITES

Official Website of Alex Morgan
www.alexmorgansoccer.com

NWSL
www.nwslsoccer.com

National Soccer Hall of Fame
www.nationalsoccerhof.com

INDEX

acting, 24, 27
assists, 11, 12, 21

basketball, 6
birthplace, 6

family, 6, 14

Golden Bears, 10, 11

headers, 4, 11

injuries, 8, 10, 26

National Women's Soccer
  League Championship, 16
national women's team, 4, 12,
  16, 18, 19, 20, 21
NCAA tournament, 10, 12

Olympics, 4, 18, 19, 25
Orlando Pride, 17

Player of the Year award, 18
political activism, 24
Portland Thorns, 16

scholarship, 8
Seattle Sounders Women, 15
softball, 6

under-20 women's national
  soccer team, 8
University of California,
  Berkeley, 8, 22

volleyball, 6, 8

Western New York Flash, 14
Women's Professional Soccer
  league, 15
Women's World Cup, 18, 22,
  23